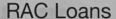

Practice Sessions

Practice Sessions

Published by BSM
in association with Virgin Books

First published in the UK in 2003 by
The British School of Motoring Ltd
1 Forest Road
Feltham
Middlesex
TW13 7RR

Second reprint 2004

ISBN 0-7535-0895-8

Design, typesetting and reprographics by Thalamus Publishing

Printed in Italy

Contents

Foreword

Every year nearly a million new learner drivers take to the road. Their aim is to gain a full driving licence. To achieve this aim and to ensure a lifetime of driving enjoyment, it is important to prepare correctly.

There is no substitute for practical experience and the best way to gain this is by taking lessons with a good professional driving instructor who uses the most up-to-date teaching techniques in a modern, dual-controlled car.

The Road Safety Strategy Document, published by the Department of Environment & Transport in March 2000, highlighted the need for a structured approach to learning to drive. Research indicates that practically every learner

who attempts the Practical Driving Test has had some professional tuition – an average of 30–35 hours of lessons. However, the research also showed that between one-third and half take no additional practice and, as a consequence, on average a novice driver only covers about 650 miles in supervised driving before taking their Test.

Because newly-qualified young drivers have a significantly higher rate of accidents in their first year on the road, it is important that they should gain as much experience as possible before taking the Test. The aim should be to try to put 'old heads on young shoulders'.

Practice Sessions has been developed by BSM in order to bring together the important aspects of learning and to make sure that the learner not only passes the Test but that their future years of driving are enjoyable and safe. The book is not a substitute for professional training but offers a template through which additional experience can be gained in a constructive way.

Formal training with a professional driving instructor and informal practice with a non-professional accompanying driver are quite different but complementary learning experiences. Learning to drive and passing the Practical Test depends on the aptitude of the individual learner together with the total amount of driving experience in both formal and informal structures.

There are no shortcuts to becoming a safe and competent motorist. Learners should not reject any opportunity for further training and experience, since their safety depends on commitment to the learning process.

Practice Sessions and its companion BSM books on both the Practical and Theory Tests give the learner the best opportunity to become a safe driver. All the books have been designed to put structure into the learning process, but at the same time they are aimed at ensuring the learner enjoys the process.

In over 90 years of teaching people to drive, BSM instructors have helped millions of people pass their Driving Test. In my view, Practice Sessions is a worthy complement to the best set of books available to help learners become safe drivers and give them a skill which will stay with them for life.

Keith Cameron
Road Safety Adviser

– Keith Cameron is one of Britain's leading authorities on motoring and driver education. He has held a number of senior positions within the Department of Transport including Chief Driving Examiner, where he had responsibility for all UK driving tests.

Introduction

For many years, BSM has recognised the benefit for learner drivers of combining a structured programme of professional tuition with opportunities for supervised private practice. Driving Instructors frequently provide informal help to those qualified drivers who choose to assist a learner by accompanying them while they practise.

However, the extent to which each individual improves as a result of private practice varies considerably. This is not simply due to the time spent practising, but also to the degree in which the private practice blends with, and is relevant to, the tuition given by the Driving Instructor. It is clear that the best results are achieved when a co-operative partnership is formed between all the parties involved.

Government statistics show that newly qualified drivers have a significantly greater chance of having an accident than more experienced drivers. This risk decreases as more miles are driven and more experience is gained. Professional tuition with a Driving Instructor is a key part of the learning process required to pass the Driving Test and develop a higher level of skill as a newly qualified driver, but practice is also extremely important. When practice is carefully structured, commenced prior to passing the Test and is supervised by an experienced driver, the risk of accidents in the early months and years of driving is significantly reduced.

This book is aimed at experienced drivers who wish to assist a learner driver gain experience through practice. However, it is not a driving instruction manual. While the book covers all aspects of the Practical Driving Test, its primary focus is to develop safer driving among newly qualified drivers, not simply to achieve a better chance of the learner passing the Test itself. It sets out a framework for a successful three-way partnership between the learner, the accompanying driver, and the Driving Instructor.

Section 1 is devoted to explaining and advising on background issues, such as the roles and responsibilities of the accompanying driver and the structure of the Practical Driving Test. Section 2 then presents a structured series of 24 practice sessions, together with advice on when to undertake them and how to plan them. Section 3 gives tables in which progress can be recorded, along with notes on particular issues.

Practice Sessions

Section 1   Your role and
responsibilities

Can you do it legally?

Once people decide that they want to learn to drive, they usually can't wait to get started. They are likely to urge you to let them have a go in your car at the earliest opportunity. But before either of you can take to the public roads together, there are a number of things that will need checking if you want to stay legal. The qualified driver and the would-be learner are jointly responsible for ensuring that you both meet the requirements.

The learner

– The minimum age at which a person is allowed to drive a car on the public roads is 17, unless you are a disabled person in receipt of mobility allowance, in which case the minimum age is 16

– Before starting to drive or applying to take the Driving Theory Test, a learner must obtain a provisional driving licence. You can get an application form from any Post Office. You may not drive until you have actually received this first licence and signed it in ink

– Your eyesight must meet the minimum standard.

– You must not take money to accompany a learner.

The accompanying driver

– You must have held a full EC/EEA driving licence for the category of vehicle being driven for at least three years

– You must be at least 21 years of age

– Unless you are an Approved Driving Instructor (ADI), you are not legally allowed to charge for giving driving lessons or for acting as an accompanying driver

– You must not accept money for fuel unless you are an Approved Driving Instructor.

Is your car suitable?

The legal requirements

The vehicle must be:

- taxed and the tax disc displayed on the nearside (left) corner of the windscreen

- insured for use by the learner and for yourself

- fitted with L-plates (D-plates in Wales) of regulation size so that they can be seen from both front and rear. (Do not put L-plates on the windscreen or rear window since they will restrict vision)

- in a roadworthy condition

- have a valid MOT Certificate if the vehicle is more than three years old.

The practical requirements

Even as an experienced driver it still takes time to get used to driving a different car to your own, since every car feels and handles differently. Bear in mind that for a learner, this lack of familiarity can be quite alarming and disorientating and it may take them some considerable time to adapt.

If your car is larger and more powerful than the one in which the learner has their driving lessons, this may cause the learner problems when judging the car's position and when carrying out manoeuvres.

– It can confuse a learner if the controls of your car are differently positioned to those of the car they drive for lessons.

It can also be a problem if the minor controls, such as indicators or windscreen wipers, are positioned in a different place. And if your car suffers minor defects, for example a weak handbrake or a stiff clutch pedal, the learner may struggle.

Remember to cover up or remove the L-plates when the vehicle is being used by a full-licence holder.

13

Are you suitable?

Before you do finally decide to take on the responsibility of accompanying a learner driver there are a number of personal factors that you may find it useful to consider.

Your own driving

The learner you accompany will, in all probability, attempt to copy the way you drive. This applies both before and after passing the Test. Nearly all of us have bad habits when driving, some more than others. If you wish to avoid causing the learner problems, it is essential that you take a look at your own driving and ensure that you still keep to the rules and follow the correct procedures.

Conflicts

Depending on how long ago you learnt to drive, you may find that the Driving Instructor has taught the learner a different technique or procedure to the one you learned and have probably always used. Advances in technology have to some extent changed experts' views on the safest way to control a car in certain situations.

If you have any doubts or worries, feel free to discuss them with the Instructor, who will be happy to explain the reasons behind any differences. You are likely to cause the learner considerable confusion if you start to argue with them or insist that they do something your way.

Inevitably, the learner will try to drive exactly as their Instructor has taught them.

Patience

To help the learner progress to being a safe driver most effectively, allow the Instructor to focus on teaching them each aspect of the syllabus and confine your role to ensuring they have ample opportunity to practise what they have been taught. Be aware that you may find this frustrating and you will be required to exercise considerable patience.

No two people learn at the same pace; while some learners master co-ordinating the controls with ease, others may take many hours of practice. Similarly, some people have great car control but find it difficult to develop road sense and risk perception.

Tension will nearly always slow a learner's progress, as will negative criticism that knocks their confidence. If you can make their practice sessions enjoyable, the learner is likely to progress much faster. So do try to be positive, and do not worry about how many times the learner gets the same thing wrong. Offer encouragement to try again, and praise even the smallest achievement.

You should also show patience with other road users, since they may not always

allow for the fact that your car is being driven by a learner.

Ensure that you have sufficient time not only to supervise the practice sessions, but also to plan them in advance. Give route directions clearly and with plenty of warning in order to give the learner time to react safely.

– Tension will nearly always slow a learner's progress, as will negative criticism.

Accompanying a learner driver

When to start accompanying a learner driver

You should check with the Instructor about when it is appropriate to start accompanying the learner on practice sessions. To a certain extent, this will depend on the ability of the learner, their level of confidence and your own, the type of car they will practise in and local geography.

In general terms, both the Driving Standards Agency and BSM advise not to start practising too early. A bad experience can destroy your confidence or that of the learner. It is certainly best to wait until the learner has a reasonable ability to use the basic controls. You may

easily create danger if the learner cannot move off, accelerate, brake and steer with reasonable fluency. These days, many tuition cars are fitted with dual controls, which makes the essential task of learning basic car control much safer than in a private vehicle.

Where to allow the learner to practise

Each of the 24 BSM Recommended Practice Sessions which follow in the next section suggest the type of road, route and traffic conditions that are likely to be appropriate. Do remember that in the early stages of learning to drive, the learner may need you to drive them somewhere safe and suitable before you

– You should not accompany a newly-qualified driver on a motorway unless they have received some form of professional tuition.

change seats and let them behind the wheel to practise.

Leaving things to the experts

Stick by the general rule that it is best to leave the Driving Instructor to take responsibility for all that is taught to the learner. Your task is to create safe and legal opportunities for the learner to practise what they have been taught. For safety reasons, there are two specific skills which BSM suggests should be left entirely to the Instructor:

Emergency stops – obviously the learner may encounter a real life situation while practising that requires them to stop in an emergency. However, practising this on a public road can be dangerous and is best left to be taught by and practised with the professional.

Motorway driving – learner drivers are not, of course, allowed on the motorway. However, when they have passed their Test, the newly-qualified driver's first trip down a motorway can be quite alarming. See page 22 for BSM's suggested action.

How to use this book – the BSM Recommended Practice System

The BSM Recommended Practice System consists of 24 practice sessions, each of which is carefully graded and structured. Each practice session is designed to complement the learner's professional driving lessons in which they will be taught specific skills. Each practice session includes suggestions for more advanced practice once the learner has mastered the basic skill.

Each practice session follows the same structure and includes the following sections:

– The skill or skills to be practised

– When and where to practise

– General safety considerations

– A note on stating the objective

– Ways of checking the learner's knowledge of the topic

– Major points to check during practice

– Suggested advanced exercises

– Common problems.

At the end of each practice session it is very helpful to both the learner and their Instructor if you:

– Discuss how things went with the learner and see if you can both agree about what went well and what went badly

– Record details of the practice session in the spaces provided towards the back of this book

– Make brief comments about progress or problems that you feel the Instructor needs to be aware of.

Pass Your Driving Test

PASS

What you should know
What you need to learn
What you must master
the Best Start in Motoring

BSM

Please note that throughout this book, reference is made to Pass Your Driving Test. This BSM publication is a fully comprehensive guide to the Practical Driving Test, which covers each area of the syllabus in detail. It is available from all good book shops, all BSM Centres, or by visiting www.bsm.co.uk.

The road to a full licence

As the accompanying driver, it is helpful for you to be familiar with the various hurdles the learner needs to overcome before gaining their full licence.

The Driving Theory Test

The learner needs to pass the Theory Test before they can apply to take the Practical Driving Test. The Theory Test nowadays comprises 2 separate elements – Multiple-Choice Questions and Hazard Perception. The learner will take the Theory Test using a computer located at the local Driving Standards Agency Theory Test Centre.

Part 1 – Multiple-Choice Questions

The question section contains 35 questions, selected from a bank of nearly 900. The candidate needs to answer at least 30 questions correctly in order to pass this section of the Test, which lasts for 40 minutes.

At the Test Centre, instructions on how to use the computer test are clearly shown and there are some practice questions to try. This first part of the Test runs on a touch-screen computer – the learner simply touches the screen to select their chosen answer or answers.

The complete Theory Test syllabus is shown on the facing page.

Part 2 - Hazard Perception

After a break of up to 3 minutes after the end of the question section, the Hazard Perception section of the Test will begin. After a tutorial video, which uses sample footage, the learner will see 14 video clips, each lasting about 1 minute. The clips feature various types of hazards, such as vehicles, pedestrians and road conditions. During each clip, the candidate is required to respond by pressing a mouse button as soon as they see a developing hazard that may result in the driver having to take some action, such as changing speed or direction. The earlier the developing hazard is spotted and a response made, the higher the score. Candidates can score up to 5 marks on each hazard and the test contains 15 hazards. In order to pass this part of the Test, the learner driver currently needs to score 44 out of 75. Note that this mark changes periodically.

Candidates are given their results when they have finished both parts of the Test and have returned to the waiting room. In order to pass the Driving Theory Test, they need to achieve a pass in both individual elements of the Test at the same sitting.

Should they fail, they must wait a minimum of three clear working days before taking the Theory Test again.

Car and motorcycle Theory Test topics

Alertness
Observation, anticipation, concentration, awareness, distraction, boredom.

Attitude
Consideration, close following, courtesy, priority.

Safety and your vehicle
Fault detection, defects and their effects on safety, use of safety equipment, emissions, noise.

Safety margins
Stopping distances, road surfaces, skidding, weather conditions.

Hazard awareness*
Anticipation, hazard awareness, attention, speed and distance, reaction time, the effects of alcohol and drugs, tiredness.

Vulnerable road users
Pedestrians, children, elderly drivers, disabled people, cyclists, motorcyclists, animals, new drivers.

Other types of vehicle
Motorcycles, lorries, buses.

Vehicle handling
Weather conditions, road conditions, time of day, speed, traffic calming.

Motorway rules
Speed limits, lane discipline, stopping, lighting, parking.

Rules of the road
Speed limits, lane discipline, parking, lighting.

Road and traffic signs
Road signs, speed limits, road markings, regulations.

Documents
Licences, insurance, MOT test certificate.

Accidents
First aid, warning devices, reporting procedures, safety regulations.

Vehicle loading
Stability, towing regulations.

*The learner's skills and understanding relating to hazard awareness are examined in greater detail by the Hazard Perception element of the Test.

Practical considerations

If the learner arrives after their appointed Test time, they will not be allowed to sit the Test. You can help the learner to avoid last-minute panics by ensuring that they have their appointment letter and have got the date and time correct.

Also check that they have an appropriate form of photographic identification, such as both parts of their signed photocard licence, their passport or some other acceptable form of identification. For obvious reasons, do not leave it until the last minute to obtain suitable proof of identity.

Studying for the Theory Test

Since no two people are the same, each learner needs to decide for themselves how they wish to go about studying for the Theory Test. Some prefer to get theory under their belt first before starting driving lessons. This is fine, but for many people it feels too much like academic hard graft, since there is no chance to link the theory to the practice. Most people seem to find it easier to study the theory and start driving lessons at the same time. The chance to put some of the theory into practice makes the theory feel more relevant and understandable.

Many learners revise for the Theory Test simply by learning the entire question bank 'parrot fashion'. Although this can be effective in achieving a Theory Test pass, this is not the best way forward. BSM recommends that a method of learning which combines studying and understanding the syllabus, then testing this understanding by practising with the actual questions gives the best chance of not only passing the Theory Test first time, but also relating the theory to the practice. BSM produces a comprehensive range of publications, including books, videos and CD-Roms which offer a complete studying solution for the Driving Theory Test.

The Practical Driving Test

The learner must bring to the Test Centre their Test appointment card, provisional driving licence and some other acceptable proof of identity that bears their name, photograph and signature.

If for any reason the learner does not intend to take the Test in their Instructor's car, it is essential that you ensure the test vehicle meets the requirements. It must display L-plates, be fitted with an extra internal mirror for use by the examiner and be in good roadworthy condition. The learner must bring the car's insurance certificate to the Test. And obviously, an appropriate qualified driver will need to accompany the learner to the Test Centre.

At the allotted time, the examiner will appear, call out the learner's name and ask them to sign against it on a form. The examiner will also ask them to show proof of identity. The examiner will then ask which car is theirs and ask them to read a car numberplate from at least the required minimum distance. If, after the examiner has measured the exact minimum distance to a numberplate, they still cannot read it, the Test will not take place and they will fail. Ensure that the candidate brings their glasses, if required.

There is now an additional section in the Practical Test, which was introduced in September 2003. This is called 'Show me, tell me'. Before getting into the car at the start of the Test, the examiner asks the candidate two questions relating to vehicle safety and maintenance.

The intention of these oral questions is to ensure that drivers know how to check that their vehicle is safe for use. While candidates will be expected to open the car's bonnet, they won't be expected to have detailed mechanical knowledge. Candidates will be asked one 'show me' and one 'tell me' question. One or both questions answered incorrectly will result in one driving fault being recorded before the candidate has even got into the driving seat.

Examples of the questions include being asked about how to check the engine oil level and tyre tread depth. The topic areas are tyres, brakes, fluids, lights, reflectors, direction indicators and horns.

After the two 'Show me, tell me' questions, the practical drive will begin. It lasts about 45 minutes. It covers various elements, many of which are discussed throughout this book. The Driving Instructor will be able to give full details.

At the end of the test

The examiner will tell the candidate whether they passed or failed. If they pass, the examiner will ask for their driving licence and give them a pass certificate. They need to send this certificate to DVLA Swansea when they

apply for their full licence. The examiner will also give them a copy of the Driving Test Report. This shows any faults that have been marked during the test so that the new driver is aware of their weaknesses and can make a conscious effort to improve.

If they fail, the examiner will give them a Statement of Failure, which will include a copy of the Driving Test Report. This will show all the faults that the examiner has marked during the Test. The examiner will also spend a few moments explaining why they failed.

After the Test

Regardless of the result, never let anyone who has just taken a Test drive away from the Test Centre; their concentration will not be at its best.

Further training

Motorways

Learner drivers are not allowed to drive on motorways, nor is motorway driving part of the driving test. BSM has campaigned for many years to get this changed, as indeed have most organisations concerned with road safety. However, the Driving Standards Agency recommends that all new drivers seek professional help from an Approved Driving Instructor before driving on a motorway.

After passing the Test, a new driver's first venture down a motorway can be very frightening. The motorway may be busy, the driver may well have forgotten some of the rules they learnt for the Theory Test, and they may find the speed of the other traffic alarming. It is not unusual to feel moments of sheer panic and fear.

BSM strongly recommends that you urge the learner you have been accompanying to take a motorway lesson with their Instructor. BSM do not advise you to accompany a new driver on a motorway unless they have received some form of professional tuition. In a car with no dual controls, you are virtually powerless to take control should anything suddenly go wrong.

Other further training

Did you know that 85% of all accidents involve some form of human error? This is the main reason why BSM offers newly-qualified drivers better protection before they take to the road.

Pass Plus

The government has introduced a scheme for newly-qualified motorists called Pass Plus. It consists of six hours of training with an Instructor and covers such skills as town, night and bad-weather driving. Completion of this course not only prepares learners even further for safe driving, but they may be entitled to reduced insurance premiums with some insurance companies, one of these being BSM Insurance Services. BSM has instructors who are specially trained to deliver Pass Plus courses.

Night Driving

If a learner does their driving during the daytime – which is when most people learn, particularly in the summer months – it is quite possible that they will gain no experience of driving in the dark. BSM offers a night-driving course, in which the instructor will show the learner how best to cope with driving in night-time conditions.

Section 2

The 24 recommended practice sessions

Session 1
Moving off and stopping on a level surface

Where and when to practise
Ideally for the first few practices you need a large, flat, empty car park, or a long, straight, level road, which is fairly wide with little traffic and not too many parked cars. Remember that unless the driving instructor has already taught the learner how to turn left, you may need to change seats with the learner in order to turn the car round and then allow practice in the opposite direction.

Changing seats too often can be frustrating and time consuming, particularly if the seat position and mirrors need to be adjusted each time you swap. For this reason, it is recommended that you do not attempt this practice too early if you cannot find a suitable road or car park.

General safety
- Avoid any road where children are playing

- Personally check that it is safe before moving off

- Make sure you are a reasonable distance from any car parked ahead of you. It should only be necessary to steer very slightly in order to reach the normal driving position

- When parking, take control of the steering wheel if necessary rather than allow your tyres to risk damage by hitting the kerb.

Explain what is to be practised and how
Check knowledge and understanding
Ask a few questions to check that the learner can remember what their driving instructor has taught them about moving off. (See Pass Your Driving Test, pages 31–36.)

Major points to check during practice
- Carries out a cockpit drill that includes doors, seat, steering, seatbelt, mirrors correctly and reasonably quickly

- Ideally for the first few practices you need a large, flat, empty car park.

- Completes safety checks before starting engine in correct sequence

- Prepares the controls of the car to be ready to move – correct gear, adequate gas, clutch at biting point and handbrake

- Observes to check it is safe, including blindspot check

- Signals if necessary

- Co-ordinates the controls smoothly as the car starts to move

- Steers adequately

- Assumes normal driving position

- Chooses a safe place to stop

- Uses Mirror, Signal, Manoeuvre (MSM) when stopping

- Brakes gently to a stop

- Positions accurately when stopped, and reasonably close to the kerb.

Advanced exercises

a) Remain on a quiet road. Use a stopwatch to time each move away and try to speed the process without any loss of control or observation. This will help when on busy roads.

b) Move off with the radio on so that the learner cannot hear the sound of the engine change when the clutch reaches biting point. This will help where other traffic noise drowns the sound of your engine.

c) Move off on slightly busier roads, practising selecting the first safe gap in the traffic.

d) Move off at traffic lights.

– Start your practice with the cockpit drill.

Common problems

Stalling:

- Lets the clutch up too far

- Sets too little gas

- Eases off the gas as the clutch comes up

- Does not keep feet still

- Releases the handbrake too late

- Kangaroo hops as the car moves off

- Feels pressure to move off quickly and loses confidence.

Stopping:

- Finds difficulty braking and steering to stop accurately

- Is unable to judge distance from the kerb

- Jolts as the car stops.

Observation:

- Takes too long between looking and moving

- Makes no blindspot check

- Uses the Mirror Signal Manoeuvre sequence incorrectly.

– Use a stopwatch to time each move away and try to speed the process.

Session 2

Using the steering wheel

Where and when to practise

There are two aspects of steering that should be practised:

1) Steering in a straight line or to keep a normal driving position on the road. This normally only requires very slight movements of the steering wheel.

2) Steering to turn a corner or manoeuvre. In this case, the steering wheel will need to be turned much further, perhaps even to full lock in one direction and then full lock in the other direction.

The first aspect can initially be practised on a quiet, reasonably straight road. The second can first be practised in an empty car park.

Learner drivers are safest practising the pull-push steering method (illustrated on the right), because once they have achieved this, they tend to find the steering required when turning corners and completing manoeuvres causes few problems. You may need to check that you understand the method and can do it yourself before you supervise your learner's practice session.

General safety

Some people find it difficult to steer in a straight line. Be ready to take control of

– Turning left – slide left hand to the top of the wheel.

– Grip and pull down with the left hand while sliding the right hand down.

– Grip and push up with the right hand while sliding the up the left hand.

– Grip and pull down with the left hand while sliding the right hand down.

– Repeat as necessary.

– Turning right – start the above with your right hand.

– Some people fid it difficult to steer in a straight line.

the steering wheel should the need arise. Having turned the steering wheel in one direction, learners often forget that they need to turn the wheel back in the opposite direction in order to straighten up. Prompt them the moment you feel they are leaving things too late. Only practise pull-push steering at slow speeds, with little or no gas, or using clutch control to keep the car slow.

Explain what is to be practised and how
Check knowledge and understanding

Ask a few questions to ensure that the learner remembers what their driving instructor has taught them about steering in a straight line and pull-push steering. (See Pass Your Driving Test, pages 28 and 30.)

Major points to check during practice

– Carries out the Cockpit Drill correctly. The correct seating position is essential in order to steer easily

– Completes safety checks before starting the engine

– Makes adequate observations to check it is safe to move off

– Gives a signal if necessary

– Keeps speed under control

– Looks well ahead and not at the bonnet or the controls

– Does not steer when the car is stopped, which can damage the tyres

- Uses smooth pull-push steering with both hands on the wheel

- Keeps both hands on the steering wheel, holding it in a suitable position

- Turns the wheel back after steering, at the correct time

- Does not cross hands on the steering wheel.

Advanced exercises

If you live near a suitable off-road centre you may be able to practise steering through slaloms. Alternatively you could book a lesson on a BSM simulator if one is available near to you.

Common problems

- Looks at the bonnet or controls and causes erratic steering

- Makes small movements of the steering wheel when large pull-push movements are needed

- Steers too much or too late

- Corrects the steering too late or not at all

- Rests right elbow on the window ledge

- Wobbles when changing gear

- Lets the steering wheel spin back.

– Keep both hands on the steering wheel and do not rest your right elbow on the window ledge.

Session 3
Clutch control

Where and when to practise
Find a quiet, reasonably straight, level road with not too many parked cars. The learner is going to practise clutch control in the way shown to them by their driving instructor. This involves making the car creep forwards as slowly as possible for a few metres and stopping again at a pre-selected point. You need to select a marker, such as a lamp-post, by which to stop the front wheels.

General safety
– Avoid any road where children may be playing

– Most of the learner's attention is likely to be focused on the clutch, so keep looking all around to ensure it is safe

– Keep a reasonable distance from the kerb and avoid driving in the gutter; the bumps will make it harder to control the car

– Do not allow the engine to over-rev for long periods of time

– Do not practise for too long at a time without a break, since the clutch might overheat

– If you do smell the clutch burning, turn off the engine and wait at least ten minutes.

Explain what is to be practised and how
The object of the exercise is to make the car move very slowly under clutch control and to stop at exact points without stalling.

Check knowledge and understanding
Ask a few questions to ensure that the learner remembers what their instructor has taught them about how the clutch works and what is happening when they use the clutch pedal. Also check that they know in which driving situations clutch control is essential. (See Pass Your Driving Test, pages 26 and 27.)

Major points to check during practice
– Completes Cockpit Drill and safety checks before starting the engine

– Selects correct gear

– Sets sufficient gas

– Finds clutch biting point

– Co-ordinates releasing the handbrake

– Carries out adequate observations

– Can control the clutch to creep forwards and stop

– Stops accurately

– Makes the car safe.

Advanced exercises

a) Try exactly the same practice but facing uphill.

b) Practise in simple driving situations where there are queues of traffic and it is necessary to keep creeping forward and stopping.

c) Imagine there is a parked car close in front; practise clutch control and steering briskly to move away around it.

d) Highlight clutch control when practising other exercises that require it, such as manoeuvres and emerging from junctions.

Common problems

– Stalls due to easing off the gas pedal

– Does not keep foot still on the clutch

– Unable to keep a very slow speed due to too much clutch movement

– Loses control of the clutch when trying to steer sharply at the same time.

How the clutch works

– The same principles apply in a four-wheel drive car.

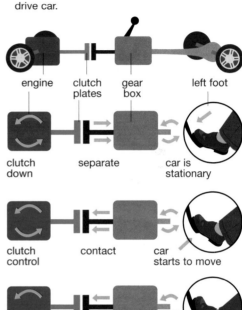

engine   clutch plates   gear box   left foot

clutch down   separate   car is stationary

clutch control   contact   car starts to move

clutch up   coupled   car is moving

Session 4
Moving off and stopping uphill

Where and when to practise
Find a quiet, reasonably wide road with ideally a fairly long and gentle uphill slope and not too many parked cars. Park just after the bottom of the hill, facing up it.

General safety
- Avoid any road where children are playing

- Personally check that it is safe before moving off

- Do not allow the learner to over-rev the engine for any length of time

- Keep an eye on the temperature gauge if practising for any length of time

- Allow the clutch to cool down between practices if biting point is held for too long

- Stop practising for at least ten minutes if you overheat the clutch.

Explain what is to be practised and how
Check knowledge and understanding
Ask a few questions to ensure the learner remembers what their driving instructor has taught them about moving off uphill. In particular, check that they understand how the clutch works and what happens as they manipulate the pedal. (See Pass

– If you smell the clutch burning, stop practising for at least ten minutes.

– The learner will soon discover that they need more gas to move off when going uphill.

Your Driving Test, pages 26–27.) Also check that the learner can remember the sequence to use when moving off uphill and what is different from moving off on a level road. (See Pass Your Driving Test, pages 33–34.)

Major points to check during practice

– Carries out Cockpit Drill correctly

– Completes safety checks before starting the engine

– Selects the correct gear

– Sets sufficient gas

– Prepares the handbrake

– Holds the clutch at biting point

– Releases the handbrake while keeping feet still

– Keeps the car still while observations are carried out, including the blind spot

– Signals if necessary

– Moves away smoothly

– Steers to normal driving position

– Uses MSM routine to stop safely

– Parks accurately and smoothly facing uphill.

Advanced exercises

a) On a quiet road use a stopwatch to encourage reducing the time it takes to move away safely.

b) Practise with the radio on so that the engine note cannot be heard.

c) Practise on busier roads to develop judgement in selecting the first safe gap in the traffic.

d) Practise on steeper hills.

e) Practise at traffic lights on hills.

Common problems

– Stalls

– Sets too little gas, or does not keep feet still when looking around

– Lets clutch up too quickly as the car moves

– Is unable to find and hold biting point

– Comes off gas too early when stopping.

– Practise starting and stopping on steeper hills.

Session 5
Moving off and stopping downhill

Where and when to practise

Find a quiet, reasonably wide road with ideally a fairly long and gentle downhill slope and not too many parked cars. Park just after the start of the hill, facing down it.

Do not park just over the brow of a hill where you might cause danger to other traffic. Most learners have little difficulty moving off safely and smoothly downhill, but they do have a tendency to forget that the way to control the car is different.

General safety

– Avoid any road where children are playing

– Personally check that it is safe before moving off

– Make sure you are a reasonable distance from any car parked ahead of you

– Do not let the learner coast downhill

– The car may move off faster than expected; be prepared to prompt the learner to use the brake.

– Be prepared – the car may move off faster than expected.

– Make sure that the learner is
  ready to use a higher gear on
  very steep hills.

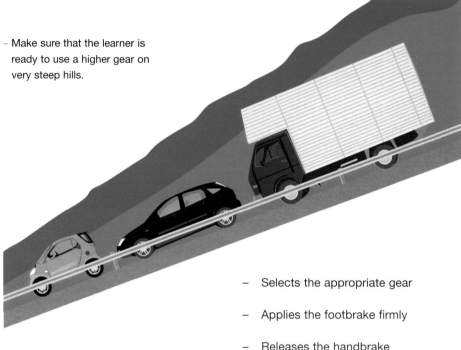

Explain what is to be practised and how
Check knowledge and understanding

Ask a few questions to check that the
learner remembers what their driving
instructor has taught them about moving
off downhill. In particular, check that the
learner understands the need to move
away using the brake to control the
speed of the car and not the clutch, the
dangers of coasting and the need to
select a higher gear on steep slopes.
(See Pass Your Driving Test, page 34.)

Major points to check during practice

– Carries out Cockpit Drill correctly

– Completes safety checks before
  starting the engine

– Selects the appropriate gear

– Applies the footbrake firmly

– Releases the handbrake

– Makes adequate observations

– Achieves smooth co-ordination
  releasing the footbrake, letting the
  clutch up smoothly and setting the
  gas, if needed

– Uses MSM to stop

– Uses the footbrake to adjust speed
  and park safely facing downhill

– Avoids coasting or riding the clutch.

Advanced exercises

a) Remain on a quiet road and use a
   stopwatch to encourage reducing the
   time it takes to move away safely.

b) Practise on busier roads to develop judgement in selecting the first safe gap in the traffic.

c) Practise on steeper hills where second gear would be appropriate.

d) Practise at traffic lights on hills.

Common problems
– Forgets the procedure

– Does not notice the car is facing downhill, causing the car to roll forward as the handbrake is released before checking it is safe to move off

– Keeps the clutch down too long and creates a jerky start

– Uses first gear on a very steep hill

– Does not brake hard enough on the downhill gradient to stop the car at the intended place.

– Ensure that the learner applies the footbrake firmly.

Session 6
Changing up to second and third gear

Where and when to practise
Ideally for the first few practices you need to find a quiet, long, straight, level road, which is reasonably wide and with not too many parked cars. Remember that unless the driving instructor has already taught the learner how to turn left, you may need to stop before the end of the road, change seats, turn the car round and continue practising in the opposite direction.

General safety
– Avoid any road where children are playing

– Personally check that it is safe before moving off

– Make sure you are a reasonable distance from any car parked ahead of you

– To start with, tell the learner when to change gear

– Do not ask the learner to change gear when too close to a parked car

– Be prepared for the car to steer to one side as the learner takes one hand off the wheel to hold the gear lever

– Make sure the car is travelling in a straight line when you ask the learner to change gear.

Explain what is to be practised and how
Check knowledge and understanding
Ask a few questions to check that the learner can remember what their driving instructor has taught them about changing gear. (See Pass Your Driving Test, pages 27–28.) With the engine off, check that they can select first, second and third

– Be prepared for the car to veer to one side as the learner takes one hand off the wheel to change gear.

Check that the learner uses the mirrors effectively.

gear using the clutch and gas correctly and without looking at the gear lever.

Major points to check during practice
- Carries out Cockpit Drill correctly

- Completes safety checks before starting the engine

- Moves off safely and smoothly

- Uses mirrors effectively

- Places hand on gear lever appropriately without looking down

- Stays in control of steering

- Pushes the clutch right down and comes off the gas at the same time

- Selects the appropriate gear

- Lets the clutch back up with a little gas

- Returns both hands to the steering wheel

- Completes the gear change before the car slows down too much

- Uses MSM to stop safely

- Parks smoothly, without stalling the engine while remaining in second or third gear.

Advanced exercises

a) Practise on a quiet road and allow the learner to decide when the speed is right to change gear.

b) Practise changing gear when going uphill.

c) Practise changing gear when going up a steep hill.

d) Practise changing gear when going downhill.

Common problems

- Looks down at the controls

- Steers off course as one hand comes off the wheel

- Selects the wrong gear

- Does not come off the gas as the clutch goes down

- Forgets to push the clutch down

- Takes too long to complete the gear change, so that the car is now travelling too slowly for the new gear.

– A common problem is looking down at the gear lever and losing control.

Session 7
Turning left from a major to a minor road

Where and when to practise

If possible, you need to choose a quiet series of level roads with good visibility where you can keep going around the block, turning and emerging to the left. If you start on a major road your first left turn will be into a minor road. The next time you turn left it will probably be into a major road. From the major road you can turn left again into a minor road and so forth until you are back where you started.

It is recommended that you do not attempt this practice session until the learner has been taught by their driving instructor both to turn left from major to minor roads and also to emerge left from minor to major roads.

General safety

– All the safety rules and procedures concerned with moving off and stopping apply to all future practice sessions and will not be listed again

– Avoid practising where cars are parked too close to the junction where you wish to turn, whether before or after the turn

– This practice is not primarily concerned with emerging from minor roads, but you need to ensure it is safe when you do so

– Be prepared to take control of the wheel when absolutely necessary.

– Learners sometimes do not correct the steering or do so too late.

– Personally check it is safe each time before you turn left

– Always be ready to prompt the learner to steer or, when absolutely necessary, to take control of the wheel yourself

– If the speed is too fast on approach, prompt the learner to slow down before it is too late.

Explain what is to be practised and how

When you first practise this exercise it is safest to be in second gear on approach to the turn.

Check knowledge and understanding

Ask a few questions to check that the learner can remember what their driving instructor has taught them. In particular, that they understand the Mirror, Signal, Position, Speed, Look (MSPSL) sequence and how to use it. (See Pass Your Driving Test, pages 43–44 and 49.)

Major points to check during practice

– Uses the mirrors effectively

– Gives correct signal at an appropriate time

– Takes up correct position before turning

– Drives at an appropriate speed on approach

– Observes before turning

– Steers sufficiently and at correct time to turn

– Does not swing out before or after turning

– Straightens wheel at the correct time

– Checks the mirrors after turning into the new road.

Advanced exercises

a) Practise on hills facing up and down.

b) Practise where there are parked cars near the junction.

c) Practise where there are pedestrians and other traffic.

d) Practise at traffic lights.

e) Practise all the above but approach in third or a higher gear and change down as appropriate.

Common problems

– Fails to check mirrors or checks mirrors and signals simultaneously

– Takes up incorrect position

– Maintains too fast a speed on approach

– Looks too late or insufficiently

– Steers too early and back wheel clips the kerb

– Steers too late and wide

– Does not correct the steering, or does so too late

– Makes no mirror check on major road

– Changes gear too late

– Does not let clutch fully up before steering.

– Make sure the learner gives the correct signals.

Session 8
Emerging left from a minor to a major road

Where and when to practise

If possible, you need to choose a quiet series of level roads with good visibility where you can keep going around the block, emerging and turning left, just as in Practice Session 7.

It is recommended that you do not attempt this practice until the learner has been taught by their driving instructor both to turn left from major to minor roads and also to emerge left from minor to major roads.

– You need to choose a quiet, level road with good visibility.

General safety

– Avoid practising where cars are parked too close to the junction where you wish to turn, whether before or after the turn

– This practice is not concerned with turning left into minor roads, but you need to ensure it is safe when you do so

– Personally check it is safe each time before you emerge

– Be especially aware that the learner may find it difficult to judge the speed of other traffic and select a safe gap

– Always be ready to prompt the learner to steer or, when absolutely necessary, to take control of the wheel yourself

– If the speed is too fast on approach, prompt the learner to slow down before it is too late.

Explain what is to be practised and how

When you first practise this exercise it is safest to be in second gear on approach. To begin with, the learner is likely to stop and select first gear before emerging, but will gradually learn to slow down and give way as appropriate.

Check knowledge and understanding

Ask a few questions to check that the learner can remember what their driving instructor has taught them about emerging left from a minor to a major road. In particular, check that they understand the different road priorities and the meaning of Give Way and Stop signs and road markings. Check that they understand the sequence Mirror, Signal, Position, Speed, Look (MSPSL) and how to use it. (See Pass Your Driving Test, pages 43–44.)

Major points to check during practice

- Uses mirrors effectively

- Gives correct signal at an appropriate time

- Takes up correct position on approach

- Adjusts speed appropriately on approach

- Observes before/during emerging

- Selects a safe gap

- Steers sufficiently and at correct time to turn

  - Positions correctly in the major road

  - Checks the mirrors after turning into the new road

  - Accelerates sufficiently on the major road to avoid causing other vehicles to slow down.

- Ask a few questions to check that the learner can remember what their driving instructor has taught them.

45

Advanced exercises

a) Practise on hills facing up and down.

b) Practise where there are parked cars near the junction.

c) Practise where there are pedestrians and other traffic.

d) Practise at closed junctions where you will need to stop.

e) Practise where visibility is very restricted and you need to edge forwards to see better.

f) Practise at open junctions where you may be able to slow down and emerge without stopping.

g) Practise all the above but approach in third or a higher gear and change down as appropriate.

Common problems

– Does not check mirrors or checks mirrors and signals simultaneously

– Takes up incorrect position

– Drives too fast on approach

– Looks too late or insufficiently

– Cannot judge a safe gap

– Stops unnecessarily when safe to keep moving

– Prepares and decides too slowly and misses gaps

– Steers too early and back wheel clips the kerb

– Straightens up too late after the turn

– Forgets the mirror check on major road

– Does not accelerate sufficiently on major road.

– Learners don't always accelerate sufficiently on major roads.

Session 9
Turning right from a major to a minor road

Where and when to practise

If possible, you need to choose a quiet set of level roads with good visibility where you can keep going round the block turning right and emerging to the right, in a similar way to Practice Session 7.

It is recommended that you do not attempt this practice until the learner has been taught by their driving instructor both to turn right from major to minor roads and also to emerge right from minor to major roads.

General safety

– This practice is not primarily concerned with emerging to the right into major roads, but you need to ensure it is safe when you do so

– Personally check it is safe each time before you turn right

– Be especially aware that the learner may find it difficult to judge the speed of oncoming traffic and select a safe gap

– Always be ready to prompt the learner to steer or, when absolutely necessary, to take control of the wheel yourself

– If the speed is too fast on approach, prompt the learner to slow down before it is too late.

Explain what is to be practised and how

When you first practise this exercise it is safest to be in second gear on approach. To begin with the learner will sometimes stop and give way to any oncoming traffic, even if there is a safe gap. They will gradually learn to slow down and turn or give way as appropriate.

– Make sure the correct position is taken up before turning right.

– The learner may not judge a safe gap.

Check knowledge and understanding

Ask a few questions to check that the learner can remember what their driving instructor has taught them about turning right from major to minor roads. In particular, check that they understand the sequence Mirror, Signal, Position, Speed, Look (MSPSL) and how to use it when turning right. (See Pass Your Driving Test, pages 43–44.)

Major points to check during practice

– Uses mirrors effectively

– Gives correct signal at an appropriate time

– Takes up correct position on approach

– Drives at an appropriate speed on approach

– Selects the correct gear

– Observes adequately on approach

– Times approach to select a safe gap or give way as necessary

– Takes up correct position before turning

– Makes a final check of right-hand mirror

– Steers sufficiently and at correct time to turn

- Positions correctly in the minor road

- Checks the mirrors after turning into the new road.

Advanced exercises

a) Practise on hills facing up and down.

b) Practise where there are no central road markings.

c) Practise where there are pedestrians and busy traffic.

d) Practise where there are queues of traffic.

e) Practise at traffic lights.

(f) Practise all the above but approach in third or a higher gear and change down as appropriate.

Common problems

- Does not check mirrors or checks mirrors and signals simultaneously

- Positions incorrectly or too late

- Drives too fast on approach
- Looks too late or insufficiently

- Cannot judge a safe gap

- Selects wrong gear or forgets to change gear

- Stops unnecessarily when safe to keep moving

- Unable to plan and time approach

- Takes too long to prepare and decide when to give way and misses gaps

- Steers too early and cuts the corner

- Forgets to check mirrors on minor road.

– The learner often forgets to change gear.

Session 10
Emerging right from a minor to a major road

Where and when to practise

If possible, you need to choose a quiet set of level roads with good visibility where you can keep going round the block emerging and turning right, just as Practice Session 8 teaches emerging and turning left.

It is recommended that you do not attempt this practice until the learner has been taught by their driving instructor both to turn right and emerge right.

General safety

– Avoid practising where visibility is poor or where parked cars restrict vision or space

– This practice is not primarily concerned with turning right into minor roads, but you need to ensure it is safe when you do so

– Personally check it is safe each time before you emerge

– Avoid practising where parked vehicles may restrict the learner's vision or space.

- Be especially aware that the learner may find it difficult to judge the speed of other traffic and select a safe gap

- If the speed is too fast on approach, prompt the learner to slow down before it is too late.

Explain what is to be practised and how

When you first practise this exercise it is safest to be in second gear on approach. To begin with the learner is likely to stop and select first gear before emerging, but will gradually learn to slow down and give way as appropriate.

Check knowledge and understanding

Ask a few questions to check that the learner can remember what their driving instructor has taught them about emerging right from minor to a major road and the particular dangers involved. In particular, check that they understand the different road priorities and the meaning of Give Way and Stop signs and road markings. Check that they understand the sequence Mirror, Signal, Position, Speed, Look (MSPSL) and how to use it. (See Pass Your Driving Test, pages 43–44.)

Major points to check during practice

- Uses mirrors effectively

- Gives correct signal at an appropriate time

- Takes up correct position on approach

- Drives at an appropriate speed on approach

- Observes and makes safe decisions before and during emerging

- Stops or gives way when necessary

- Selects a safe gap

- Steers sufficiently and at correct time to turn

- Positions correctly in the major road

- Checks the mirrors after turning into the new road

- Accelerates sufficiently on the major road to avoid causing other vehicles to slow down.

Advanced exercises

a) Practise on hills facing up and down.

b) Practise where there are parked cars near the junction.

c) Practise where there are pedestrians and busy traffic.

d) Practise at closed junctions where you will need to stop.

e) Practise where visibility is very restricted and you need to edge forwards to see better.

– Practise where there are pedestrians and busy traffic.

f) Practise at open junctions where you may be able to slow down and emerge without stopping.

g) Practise all the above but approach in third or a higher gear and change down as appropriate.

Common problems

– Does not check mirrors or checks mirrors and signals simultaneously

– Takes up incorrect position

– Drives too fast on approach

– Looks too late or insufficiently

– Cannot judge a safe gap

– Stops too far back or forward

– Stops unnecessarily when safe to keep moving

– Prepares and decides too slowly and misses gaps

– Steers too early or late

– Forgets mirror check on major road

– Does not accelerate sufficiently on major road.

Session 11
Changing up and down through all the gears

Where and when to practise
You need to find a road or series of roads that are reasonably straight and level without much traffic. One road with a speed limit over 30mph would be useful. It is recommended that, as you will be travelling much faster, you do not attempt this practice with the learner unless Practice Session 6 has already been completed satisfactorily.

General safety
–   To start with, you may need to prompt the learner when to change gear

– To start with you may need to prompt the learner to change gear.

–   Do not ask the learner to change gear when too close to a parked car

–   Be ready for the car to steer to one side as the learner takes a hand off the wheel to hold the gear lever. You practised this in Session 6, but the car will now be travelling much faster

–   Make sure the car is travelling in a straight line when you ask the learner to change gear

–   Make sure it is safe behind particularly before the learner slows down and changes down

–   Take great care that first gear is not selected by mistake at high speed.

Explain what is to be practised and how
The learner will be practising changing up and down through all the gears while travelling along a straight road.
They are doing this to gain fluency and smoothness at gear changing and to get used to the speeds appropriate for each

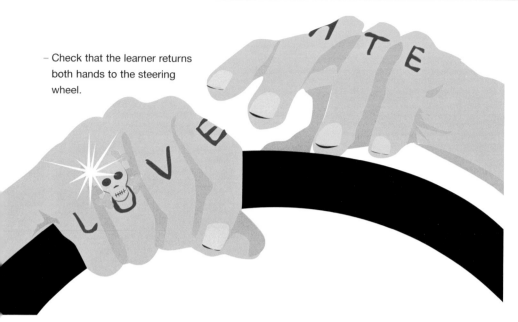

– Check that the learner returns both hands to the steering wheel.

gear. The learner must not slow down and change down when other traffic is behind you on an open road, as you will not be expected to act like this. Remember this is simply practice and not how you would normally drive.

Check knowledge and understanding

Ask a few questions to check that the learner can remember what their driving instructor has taught them about changing gear. (See Pass Your Driving Test, pages 27–28.) With the engine off, check that they can select each gear in sequence both up and down, without looking at the gear lever.

Major points to check during practice

– Checks the mirrors

– Places hand on gear lever appropriately; does not look down

– Keeps steering in control

– Pushes the clutch right down and comes off the gas at the same time

– Selects the appropriate gear for the speed

– Lets the clutch back up with a little gas

– Returns both hands to the steering wheel

– Completes the gear change up before the car slows down too much

– Brakes sufficiently before selecting the next gear down.

Advanced exercises

a) Remain on a quiet road and allow the learner to decide without any prompts when the speed is right to change gear both up and down.

b) Practise changing gear up and down when going uphill.

c) Practise changing gear up and down when going up a steep hill.

d) Practise changing gear when going downhill.

e) Practise block gear changing both up and down.

f) Practise braking in the high gears and selecting first gear while the car is still moving slowly.

Common problems

– Looks down at the controls

– Steers off course as one hand comes off the wheel

– Selects the wrong gear by mistake

– Selects the wrong gear for the speed and conditions

– Does not come off the gas as the clutch goes down

– Forgets to push the clutch down

– Takes too long to complete a gear change up so that the car is now travelling too slowly for the new gear selected

– Does not slow down enough before changing down.

– Take great care that the first gear is not selected at high speed.

Session 12
Moving off at an angle

Where and when to practise

Both the learner and the person accompanying them can feel nervous when practising this exercise due to the close proximity of the other vehicle. Before attempting this practice you may wish to imagine a parked car ahead and check the learner's confidence by carrying out the practice and moving out around the pretend car. Alternatively you could position a tall cone or other marker in a quiet road to represent the off-side rear of a parked car.

It is recommended that you do not attempt this practice until the learner can move off fluently on a level road and is confident with clutch control. Their driving instructor will be able to advise when they are ready.

Before you start this session, find a quiet, level road which is reasonably wide with sufficient gaps between the parked cars to allow the learner to park about a car length behind the vehicle in front.

General safety

– Avoid any road where children are playing

– Personally check that it is safe before moving off

– Be sensitive to the owners of parked cars – your L-plates may make them apprehensive as they see the learner get closer and closer to their dream car.

- Keep looking all around as the car starts to move

- Look particularly for oncoming traffic into whose path the learner might pull out

- Be aware that the learner may not correct the steering quickly enough and finish positioned too wide or on the wrong side of the road

- Be sensitive to the owners/drivers of parked cars – your L-plates may make them apprehensive as they see the learner get closer and closer to their dream car.

Explain what is to be practised and how

The objective is to move off safely and under control around the parked car in front, drive a short distance and park again on the left somewhere safe and suitable to try again.

Check knowledge and understanding

Ask a few questions to check that the learner can remember what their driving instructor has taught them about moving off at an angle. Check in particular that they recognise the need to use the clutch to control speed and the need to allow time to steer; and check also that they are aware of the necessity for frequent observations all around. (See Pass Your Driving Test, pages 34–35.)

Major points to check during practice

- Prepares the controls of the car to be ready to move – correct gear, adequate gas, clutch at biting point and handbrake

- Observes to check it is safe, including blind spot check

- Signals if necessary

- Achieves slow speed with clutch control

- Maintains smooth co-ordination as the car starts to move

- Steers briskly

- Corrects steering to achieve normal driving position

- Selects a safe place to stop

- Uses Mirror, Signal, Manoeuvre (MSM) when stopping

- Brakes gently to a stop

- Positions accurately when stopping by the kerb.

Advanced exercises

a) Remain on a quiet road, and gradually reduce the gap from the parked car in front.

b) Practise on slightly busier roads, attempting to take advantage of the

– It is a common problem that the learner fails to notice oncoming traffic.

first safe gap in the traffic.

c) Practise on an uphill gradient.

d) Practise on a downhill gradient where brake control will be necessary.

Common problems

- Stalls because of the need to steer more than usual

- Moves off too fast to steer sufficiently due to poor clutch control

- Steers too gently

- Jerks due to poor clutch control

- Observes inadequately, especially not looking several times as the car edges out

- Fails to notice oncoming traffic

- Corrects the steering too late and finishes up too wide.

Session 13
Reversing around a corner to the left

Where and when to practise

Find a quiet junction where the roads are level, with no parked cars in the vicinity of the corner around which the learner will practise reversing. The corner should be reasonably sharp, nearly a right angle. You may find it useful to check that the learner can reverse slowly in a straight line, for a reasonable distance, before you attempt this practice. Their driving instructor will have taught them both this and the left reverse, but the change to a different car can sometimes cause problems.

– Avoid corners where a tree or postbox is near the kerb or obstructs vision.

General safety

– Avoid corners where a tree or post-box is near the kerb or obstructs vision

– Avoid any road junctions where children are playing

– Personally check that it is safe just before the car starts to reverse

– Keep checking all around as the car starts to move

– Check particularly for oncoming traffic as the learner begins to steer because the front of the car will swing out

Explain what is to be practised and how

Stop in the major road before the corner which the learner is going to reverse around. This allows them to assess the corner and then to drive past it and stop in a suitable position to start the practice.

Check knowledge and understanding

Ask a few questions to check that the learner can remember what their driving instructor has taught them about reversing to the left. (See Pass Your Driving Test, pages 94–95.)

– The learner should reverse reasonably close to the kerb.

Major points to check during practice

– Positions safely and suitably in order to commence the reverse

– Looks into turning for any problems

– Prepares to reverse correctly, including seating position and grip on steering wheel

– Looks all around before the car moves

– Looks back over left shoulder while reversing in a straight line towards the corner with frequent glances to the front

– Checks all round before steering and especially over right shoulder before the front of the car swings out

– Keeps reasonably close to the kerb

– Looks over left shoulder having rounded the corner with frequent glances to the front

– Uses clutch to control speed throughout the exercise unless going downhill

– Continues to reverse in a straight line for a reasonable distance and stops safely

– Gives way to other traffic or pedestrians as necessary.

Advanced exercises

a) Practise on corners which are long, gentle curves, not right angles.

– The learner should check all around before steering.

60

b) Practise reversing uphill around corners.

c) Practise reversing downhill around corners.

d) Practise around corners where the start road is level or slightly uphill as you reverse and changes to sharply downhill as you reverse into the new road.

e) Practise on corners where there are no kerbstones to help judge the position.

– Make sure the learner is prepared to give way to pedestrians.

Common problems

– Observes inadequately and especially fails to check to the front and sides before steering

– Does not notice other vehicles and does not give way

– Reverses too fast and not in control

– Starts too close to the kerb, too near to the corner or not parallel to the kerb

– Steers too early or late

– Corrects steering too early or late to maintain position.

Session 14
Reversing around a corner to the right

Where and when to practise
Find a quiet junction where the roads are level, with no parked cars in the vicinity of the corner around which the learner will practise reversing. The corner should be reasonably sharp, nearly a right angle. It is recommended that the learner does not attempt this practice until they can reverse to the left with confidence.

General safety
– Avoid corners where a tree or post-box is near the kerb or obstructs vision

– Avoid any road where children are playing

– Personally check that it is safe just before the car starts to reverse

– Keep checking all around as the car starts to move

– Check particularly for oncoming traffic as the learner begins to steer since the front of the car will swing out

– Remember that you are actually reversing on the wrong side of the road in the path of oncoming traffic. Frequent forward checks are needed. Once round the corner, always reverse back until you are well clear of the junction – about six car lengths.

– Reverse back until well clear of the junction.

Explain what is to be practised and how

Stop on the left in the major road before the corner which the learner is going to reverse around. This allows them to assess the corner and, when safe, move off, cross to the right side of the road and park beyond the junction in a suitable position from which to reverse around it.

Check knowledge and understanding

Ask a few questions to check that the learner can remember what their driving instructor has taught them about reversing to the right. (See Pass Your Driving Test, pages 96–97.)

– Make sure that the learner is still prepared to give way to pedestrians.

Major points to check during practice

– Positions safely and suitably in order to commence the reverse

– Looks into turning for any problems

– Prepares to reverse correctly, including seating position and grip on steering wheel

– Looks all around before the car moves

– Looks over right shoulder when reversing to the corner with frequent glances to the front

– Checks all round before steering

– Keeps reasonably close to the kerb

– Looks over right shoulder, having rounded the corner with frequent glances to the front

– Uses clutch to control speed throughout the exercise unless going downhill

– Continues to reverse in a straight line for a reasonable distance and stops safely well back from the junction

– Gives way to other traffic or pedestrians as necessary.

Advanced exercises

a) Practise on corners which are long, gentle curves, not right angles.

b) Practise reversing uphill around corners.

c) Practise reversing downhill around corners.

d) Practise around corners where the start road is level or slightly uphill as you reverse and changes to sharply downhill as you reverse into the new road.

e) Practise on corners where there are no kerbstones to help judge the position.

Common problems

– Observes inadequately, especially failing to check to the front often enough and before steering

– Does not notice other vehicles and does not give way

– Reverses too fast and is not in control

– Starts too close to the kerb, too near to the corner or not parallel to the kerb

– Steers too early or too late

– Loses control when correcting the steering and fails to maintain position.

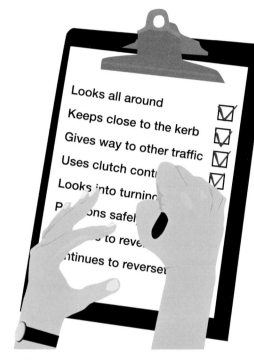

Looks all around
Keeps close to the kerb ☑
Gives way to other traffic ☑
Uses clutch contr ☑
Looks into turning ☑
P ᴐns safel
ᴐ to reve.
ntinues to reverse

– Make sure you check all the major points during practice.

Session 15
Turning the car in the road

Where and when to practise
Find a quiet and fairly wide, level road, preferably with a reasonably gentle camber. Park on the left, well away from parked cars on either side of the road and any trees or other obstacles close to the kerb.

General safety
–   Avoid conducting this practice where a tree or post-box is near the kerb and would be immediately in front or behind as you drive across the road and reverse back

– Avoid any road where children are playing.

–   Avoid any road where children are playing

–   Personally check that it is safe throughout the manoeuvre

–   Check particularly for other traffic, and when necessary advise the learner to give way

–   Do not drive or reverse towards pedestrians on the pavement

–   If other traffic waves at the learner to continue, be sure they really mean it

–   Be aware that another car waiting puts pressure on the learner and may cause them to stall.

Explain what is to be practised and how
The learner is going to turn the car around in the road by means of forward and reverse gears and then park on the left.

Check knowledge and understanding
Ask a few questions to check that the learner can remember what their driving instructor has taught them about the turn in the road. (For a full account see Pass Your Driving Test, pages 99–106.)

Major points to check during practice
–   Parks safely and suitably in order to commence the manoeuvre

–   Looks all around before the car moves

65

– Check that the learner waits for any traffic to pass.

– Waits for any traffic to pass

– Looks in appropriate directions to check it is safe throughout the manoeuvre

– Controls the speed

– Steers briskly and steers back at the appropriate time

– Applies the handbrake when stopped at the end of each phase of the manoeuvre

– Maintains control and does not roll forwards or back on the camber

– Avoids touching the kerb

– Parks safely at the end of the manoeuvre.

Advanced exercises

a) Practise on increasingly narrow roads.

b) Practise on roads where some other traffic is likely to pass during the manoeuvre.

c) Practise on hills facing up at the start of the manoeuvre.

d) Practise on hills facing down at the start of the manoeuvre.

e) Practise on roads with a steep camber.

Common problems

– Observes inadequately, too long before the car moves, not in the direction the car is moving, or for too long in one direction

– Fails to notice other vehicles and does not give way

– Does not notice pedestrians

– Ensure that the learner doesn't take excessive time to complete the manoeuvre and holds up traffic.

– Drives forward or reverses too fast and not in control

– Fails to steer the other way as the car nears the kerb

– Hits or mounts the kerb

– Does not switch from clutch control to the foot brake on a steep camber and loses control

– Takes excessive time to complete the manoeuvre and holds up the traffic.

Session 16
Reversing into a parking space

Where and when to practise
Find a car park where at least one section is reasonably quiet and which has clearly marked parking bays. Initially you may find it less stressful to choose a bay for the learner to park in with another car on one side only and without another occupied bay or a brick wall immediately behind it.

General safety
– Keep a continuous lookout for other vehicles and pedestrians

– Stop the practice and start again if things start to go terribly wrong

– Do not allow the learner to get too close to any other vehicles.

Explain what is to be practised and how
Stop in the car park somewhere safe, in a position where you can point out the bay into which you want the learner to reverse. In that way, they will be able to drive to a suitable position from which to reverse.

Check knowledge and understanding
Ask a few questions to check that the learner can remember what their driving instructor has taught them about reverse-parking into a parking bay. In particular, check that they understand the need for all-round continuous observation and the need to keep the car under control and moving slowly. (See Pass Your Driving Test, page 114.)

Major points to check during practice
– Positions safely and suitably in order to commence the reverse

– Prepares to reverse correctly, including seating position and grip on steering wheel

– Find a car park where at least one section is reasonably quiet and which has clearly marked parking bays.

– Make sure that the learner does not protrude unnecessarily at the front.

- Looks all around before the car moves

- Looks mainly over left shoulder when reversing, with frequent glances all around

- Checks all round before steering and swinging to left or right

- Reverses slowly under clutch control

- Does not steer too much or too little

- Stops within the parking bay

- Stops parallel to the white lines and a reasonable distance from any car to either side

- Stops before any obstruction to the rear of the vehicle

- Does not protrude unnecessarily from the front of the parking bay.

Advanced exercises

a) Practise in a busier car park.

b) Practise with an obstruction behind the parking bay and cars parked on both sides.

c) Practise where limited space makes it difficult to find a position from which to reverse easily.

d) Practise in a car park where the bays are narrower than normal.

e) Practise reversing into a parking bay from the right.

Common problems

– Attempts to reverse into the parking bay at right angles instead of drawing forwards at an angle and trying to reverse back as straight as possible

– Observes inadequately, especially failing to check all around before reversing and all the time the car is moving

– Looks out of the right-hand window to see the white lines at the expense of all-round observation

– Does not notice other vehicles or pedestrians and does not give way

– Reverses too fast and not in control

– Turns the steering wheel too much

– Parks outside the white lines

– Parks too far forward or back in the bay.

– Do not allow the learner to get too close to any other vehicles.

Session 17
Reverse parking

Where and when to practise
Find a quiet, level road with a parked car which has a long gap behind it of at least three car lengths or no other car at all. Stop and park further back down the road in a position from which both you and the learner can see the gap into which you intend the learner to reverse.

General safety
– Keep a continuous lookout for other vehicles and pedestrians

– Make sure you are not too near a bend or the brow of a hill

– Avoid roads where children are playing

– Do not choose a place that would block someone's driveway or narrow the road too much

– Be sure that it is legal to park there

– Avoid hills or steeply cambered roads for first attempts at this exercise

– Stop the practice and start again if

things begin to go terribly wrong

– Do not allow the learner to get too close to any other vehicles.

Explain what is to be practised and how
By stopping further back down the road, the learner has a chance to study the gap into which you wish them to reverse and to assess the situation. This will also allow the learner to drive off and stop safely, positioned in a suitable place from which to commence the reverse-park.

– Find a quiet, level road with a parked car which has a long gap behind it of at least three car lengths.

Check knowledge and understanding

Ask a few questions to check that the learner can remember what their driving instructor has taught them about reverse parking. In particular, check that they understand the need for good all-round continuous observation and the need to keep the car under control and moving slowly. (See Pass Your Driving Test, pages 107–115.)

Major points to check during practice

– Warns other drivers of the intention, by giving an early signal if necessary

– Positions safely and suitably in order to commence the reverse

– Prepares to reverse correctly, including seating position and grip on steering wheel

– Looks all around before the car moves

– Looks mainly over left shoulder when reversing, with frequent glances all around

– Checks all round before steering left, which brings the rear end of the car in, but swings the front end out into the road

– Reverses slowly under clutch control

– Does not steer too much or too little

– Does not hit the kerb

– Stops parallel to the kerb and reasonably close to it.

Advanced exercises

a) Practise on busier roads

b) Practise reversing into a smaller gap, but never less than one and a half car lengths.

c) Practise on hills both up and down.

– Never try to reverse into a gap of less than one and a half times the length of your car.

d) Practise on a road with a very steep camber.

e) Practise reversing into a gap on the right-hand side of the road. Either choose a very quiet road or a quiet one-way street.

Common problems

– Stops too close to the car at the start of the exercise

– Observes inadequately before starting to reverse

– Makes no frequent checks ahead and all around

– Fails to look around before steering left

– Does not notice other vehicles or pedestrians and does not give way

– Goes too fast and is not in control

– Turns the steering wheel too much

– Straightens the wheels too late, the result being that the front of the car mounts the kerb

– Finishes up too far from the kerb.

Session 18
Dealing with roundabouts

Where and when to practise
In order to practise this session efficiently it is best to try and find two or more roundabouts that are reasonably close together. You can then plan a series of routes that allow the learner to approach from different directions and exit to the left, right and straight ahead.

You can also go all the way round the roundabout, double back on yourself and approach the previous roundabout from the opposite direction. Ideally, the roundabouts should have four entrances and exits, and two or more lanes approaching and leaving.

– Check that the learner uses MSPSL correctly on approach.

General safety
– Learners sometimes stop at a roundabout when the vehicle behind expects them to keep moving; keep a close look behind

– When stopped behind another car at a roundabout, learners may keep looking right, see a gap, and go without looking ahead; the car in front may not have moved, so beware

– Personally check it is safe each time the learner joins a roundabout

- The learner may misjudge the speed of traffic on the roundabout and not select a safe gap

- If the speed is too fast on approach, prompt the learner to slow down before it is too late.

Explain what is to be practised and how

The learner will practise approaching roundabouts and exiting to the left, right and straight ahead.

Check knowledge and understanding

Ask a few questions to check that the learner can remember what their driving instructor has taught them about roundabouts, their purpose and the particular dangers involved. Check that they understand who has priority, how to approach, position and signal and how to use lane discipline for the different exits they will take. Check that they remember the sequence Mirror, Signal, Position, Speed, Look (MSPSL) and how to use it. (See Pass Your Driving Test, pages 43–44.)

Major points to check during practice

- Uses MSPSL correctly on approach

- Anticipates a safe gap and adjusts speed to keep moving when possible

- Gives way when necessary

- Selects the correct lane for the exit being taken

- Signals correctly on approach, when on the roundabout and for the exit to be taken

- Checks blindspot and signals before changing lanes

- Keeps space from large vehicles, horse riders and bicycles.

Advanced exercises

a) Practise on busy roundabouts.

b) Practise on roundabouts with more than four exits.

c) Practise on roundabouts where the normal give-way rules are changed by the road markings.

d) Practise on very large roundabouts which are one-way gyratory traffic systems and have many lanes, direction arrows on the lanes and many different direction signs and exits.

e) Practise on small roundabouts with only one lane at each entrance and exit.

f) Practise on mini-roundabouts.

Common problems

- Uses MSPSL too late on approach

- Positions in incorrect lane on approach

- Approaches at too fast a speed

- Hesitates or stops when safe to go

- When stopped, prepares and decides too slowly and misses gaps

- Signals incorrectly or too early or too late

- Takes incorrect lane on roundabout for the exit chosen

- Does not stay in lane

- Does not look before changing lanes and cuts up other vehicles.

- Try to get the learner to practise on a busy roundabout.

Session 19
Dealing with pedestrian crossings

Where and when to practise
In order to practise this session efficiently, try to find a number of pedestrian crossings that are reasonably close together. You can then plan a series of routes that allow the learner to approach from different directions. You will need to provide the learner with experience of all the different types of pedestrian crossing, including those controlled by light signals.

General safety
– Pedestrians are vulnerable and you need to take great care

– Watch out particularly for pedestrians and children on the pavement, running in the direction of the crossing and with their backs to you; they may cross without looking

– Try to personally spot each crossing as far ahead as possible so that you can judge if the learner is acting appropriately

– If the learner approaches a crossing too fast and pedestrians are nearby, give an early warning to slow down

– Keep a careful watch for vehicles

close behind who may not expect the learner to slow down or stop

– Never wave pedestrians across the road or allow the learner to do so.

Explain what is to be practised and how
The learner will practise approaching both controlled and uncontrolled crossings, spotting them well ahead, using MSPSL, giving way when appropriate and obeying light signals.

– Pedestrians and children are vulnerable, so watch out. They may cross without looking to see what's coming.

Ask a few questions to check that the learner can remember what their driving instructor has taught them about the different types of pedestrian crossing, how to deal with them and the dangers involved. Check that they understand the rules that govern different types of crossing and when, where and for whom they must stop by law or should stop to be safe and courteous. Check that they remember the sequence Mirror, Signal, Position, Speed, Look (MSPSL) and how to use it. Ask them to demonstrate a slowing-down arm signal and suggest when they might need to use it. (See Pass Your Driving Test, pages 123–128.)

- Spots the crossing far enough ahead

- Uses MSPSL early enough and correctly on approach

- Anticipates actions of pedestrians and shows consideration

- Slows down, gives way or stops when necessary

- Anticipates traffic signals and obeys them

- Ask a few questions to check that the learner can remember what their driving instructor has taught them about the different types of pedestrian crossing.

78

– Gives slowing-down arm signal when needed

– Checks it is safe before moving off

– Makes progress and does not hold up other traffic unnecessarily.

Advanced exercises

a) Practise dealing with crossings that have a central island, both controlled and uncontrolled, staggered and straight.

b) Practise where there are two lanes on approach to a crossing.

c) Practise where there is a continual stream of pedestrians wanting to cross.

d) Practise in the dark, when pedestrians are harder to see.

e) Practise near schools at the beginning and end of the day to gain experience of school-crossing patrols.

– Practise where there is a continual stream of pedestrians.

Common problems

– Spots the crossing too late

– Fails to anticipate actions of pedestrians, resulting in harsh, last-minute braking

– Uses MSPSL too late on approach

– Gives way unnecessarily

– Moves off without checking it is safe to do so

– Fails to anticipate light signals and brakes harshly to stop

– Remains stationary at an amber flashing light even if the crossing is clear.

Session 20
Meeting other traffic

Where and when to practise
Meeting other traffic is the term used to describe a situation where the road is narrowed to less than the width of two vehicles and there is a vehicle approaching you from the opposite direction. Since you will both be using the same space this is a hazard. Try to find a series of narrow roads or, more likely, roads that are narrowed because cars are parked on both sides.

General safety
– Be personally aware of the space to both sides and behind as well as the space in front; less space means less speed. Ask the learner to slow down if necessary, before things get out of hand

– Look ahead for gaps between parked cars, and be ready to point out a suitable place for the learner to pull in and give way. This is safer than finding that the learner needs to reverse because they have not made use of MSM or planned for oncoming vehicles

– Do not assume that the oncoming vehicle will give way just because the parked cars or other obstructions are on their side of the road

– Take particular care if there is a vehicle close behind.

– Check that the learner remembers what is meant by 'meeting other traffic'.

Explain what is to be practised and how
The learner will practise meeting other traffic in roads where either the learner or the oncoming vehicle will need to select a suitable gap to pull into and give way.

Check knowledge and understanding
Ask a few questions to check that the learner can remember what their driving instructor has taught them about meeting other traffic. Ask them to explain how they will use MSM when meeting other traffic. Find out what they understand by anticipation and why they think it is important in this situation. Also ask what

factors they will consider when deciding whether to keep going or give way. (See Pass Your Driving Test, pages 83–85.)

Major points to check during practice
- Reduces speed early when the road narrows or is narrowed by obstructions

- Looks well ahead for oncoming vehicles

- Reduces speed early enough to make a decision to go or give way

- Looks for gaps to pull into and give way

- Leaves enough room to pull out of the gap when safe

- Normally gives way when the obstruction is on the learner's side of the road

- Look well ahead for gaps between parked cars.

- Notices passing places on narrow country lanes

- Does not hesitate unduly.

Advanced exercises
a) Practise on hills both up and down.

b) Practise in the dark when the learner may find it harder to judge space, distance and the speed and size of an oncoming vehicle.

c) Practise on busier side roads where there may be a stream of traffic in both directions.

d) When possible practise in bad weather conditions, such as when it is raining.

Common problems
- Fails to observe developing situations sufficiently far ahead

- Does not use MSM or fails to use it early enough, causing late braking or a need to stop and reverse

- Hesitates, unable to decide whether to keep going

- Waves the oncoming driver on

- Pulls into a gap and stops too close to a parked car or obstruction in front.

Session 21
Dealing with dual carriageways

Where and when to practise

It is safest to start by finding a dual carriageway, not too busy and with two lanes in each direction. Initially, choose a place to join where there is an acceleration lane and a place to leave where there is a deceleration lane. This makes it much easier for the learner to practise joining and leaving.

General safety

- The learner may have had very limited practice to date of travelling at speeds of up to 70mph; you need to be even more vigilant than usual

- If the learner finds difficulty staying in lane, end the practice as soon as it is safe; this may be due to the change from the driving instructor's car to yours

- Make frequent checks in your extra mirror, especially before asking the learner to change lanes, turn left or right or overtake

– Start by finding a dual carriageway, not too busy and with two lanes in either direction.

- Personally check the blindspot before changing lanes

- Do not allow the learner to drive too close to the vehicle in front

- Only overtake when there is ample time and space.

Explain what is to be practised and how

The learner will practise joining, leaving and driving on dual carriageways, keeping pace with the traffic at up to the speed limit, looking well ahead, keeping space, lane discipline and simple overtaking.

– Do not allow the learner to drive too close to the vehicle in front.

Check knowledge and understanding

Ask a few questions to check that the learner can remember what their driving instructor has taught them about driving on dual carriageways. Make sure they understand what they should do to join and leave, can use the two-second rule, and know how to use MSM to change lanes. (See Pass Your Driving Test, pages 73 and 80–83.)

Major points to check during practice

- Uses any acceleration or deceleration lane appropriately to join or leave

- Joins and leaves safely where there is no acceleration or deceleration lane

- Drives in the centre of the lane

- Complies with lane discipline

- Keeps adequate space all around and especially in front

- Uses MSM to change lanes

- Changes lanes smoothly

- Overtakes safely if required

- Does not drive too slowly and hold up the traffic, nor break the speed limit.

Advanced exercises

a) Practise joining and leaving where there are no acceleration or deceleration lanes.

b) Practise turning right onto a dual carriageway where there is a wide, central reservation.

c) Practise turning right onto a dual carriageway where there is a narrow central reservation.

d) Practise in the dark and in bad weather.

– Steers too harshly when changing lanes

– Drives too close to the vehicle in front

– Drives too slowly

– Brakes in left-hand lane, when turning left, rather than waiting and using the deceleration lane to slow down.

– Ensure that the learner drives in the middle of the lane.

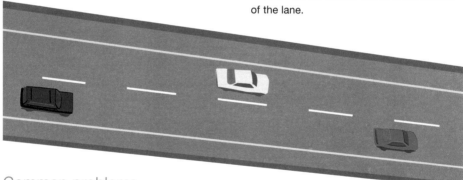

Common problems

– Builds up speed too slowly on the acceleration lane

– Does not observe developing situations sufficiently far ahead

– Fails to use MSM, or does not use it early enough

– Does not drive in the centre of the lane

84

Session 22
Commentary driving

Where and when to practise

This Practice Session has two elements. In the first, you will drive and the learner will give a commentary from the passenger seat. In the second, the learner will both drive and give a commentary. This will help you establish exactly what the learner is looking at and what they see as important when driving, and will enable you to focus further practice on the risky situations that you feel the learner is failing to take into account.

To start with you need to plan short routes, which take perhaps five or ten minutes to drive around and which have varied road and traffic conditions.

You may find it beneficial to repeat the same route several times.

General safety

– When you are driving, do not allow yourself to become over-distracted by the learner's commentary

– When the learner is driving and giving a commentary, their driving may suffer initially from the extra mental effort needed

– Start by simply asking the learner to point out risks they can see; gradually build on this so that they also predict potential problems and finally include what action they are taking

– You may find it beneficial to repeat the same route several times.

- Avoid attempting this exercise for more than a few minutes at a time in the early stages.

– Ask the learner to predict potential problems.

Explain what is to be practised and how

First, you will drive and the learner will point out all the risks they perceive to be a problem. Then the learner will practise driving for short periods, in varied conditions, stating the risks they see as important and detailing what action they are taking to deal with them safely. Regardless of who is driving, the amount of detail that you ask the learner to give as a commentary should be built up gradually.

Check knowledge and understanding

Ask a few questions to check the learner can remember what their driving instructor has taught them about developing commentary driving. Discuss the need for total concentration and avoiding distractions. They will understand the task far easier if they have read Pass Your Driving Test, pages 131–136 and pages 145–152.

Major points to check during practice

- Looks well ahead for possible problems

- Selects appropriate problems on which to comment

- Proposes actions which are safe, well-timed and appropriate

- Maintains a high level of concentration

- Demonstrates all-round awareness through their commentary

- Maintains control of the car to a reasonably high standard.

Advanced exercises

a) Practise for longer periods of time as concentration improves.

b) Increase the amount of detail in the commentary.

c) Practise on country roads.

d) Practise in the dark.

Common problems

– Distracted by giving a commentary at the same time as driving

– Initially embarrassed at speaking out loud

– Lacks concentration

– Focuses too much attention on one problem

– Has difficulty anticipating what might happen next

– Can't see any risk

– Can't decide what to do

– Spots a risk too late or takes too long to act.

– The learner may become distracted from driving by giving a commentary.

Session 23
Night driving

Where and when to practise
This Practice Session is divided into two tasks. The first involves practising driving at dusk and at night, in built-up areas and on other roads where there are street lights. Try to plan a route that involves a variety of well-lit main roads and more poorly-lit back streets.

The second task requires the learner to practise driving on unlit roads. Plan a suitable route to include major two-way roads, dual carriageways and narrower country lanes. At least one practice for each element should start just before dusk, so that the learner can decide when to turn on the headlights and become familiar with the difficulty of seeing other vehicles that have no lights switched on.

– Try to plan a route that involves a variety of well-lit or more poorly-lit streets.

General safety
– Remind the learner to turn on the headlights if they fail to do so when necessary

– Do not allow the learner to dazzle other drivers

– Be ready to steady the wheel if the learner is dazzled by oncoming traffic

– Pay particular attention to speed, especially when passing oncoming traffic and approaching bends

– Watch out for cyclists and

pedestrians who may be hidden in the gloom

- Take care at junctions where the speed of other traffic may be hard to judge.

Explain what is to be practised and how

The learner will practise turning on the headlights at the appropriate time, and then using dipped and full-beam lights, dipping headlights correctly and judging speed, space and visibility in the dark.

Check knowledge and understanding

Ask a few questions to check that the learner can remember what their driving instructor has taught them about the extra dangers of driving in the dark. In particular, check that they can operate the light controls easily and know when and how to dip their headlights and return to full beam. (See Pass Your Driving Test, pages 153–156.)

Major points to check during practice

- Switches on dipped headlights when required

- Uses full beam headlights on unlit roads when safe to do so

- Avoids dazzling other road users and dips the lights when necessary and at the right moment

- Adjusts speed to match conditions and visibility

- Judges the speed of other traffic accurately

- Judges space and distance accurately

- Takes appropriate action when dazzled by another vehicle.

– Watch out for cyclists in the gloom.

Advanced exercises

a) Practise at busy, complex junctions and roundabouts.

b) Practise joining and crossing dual carriageways with a reasonable flow of traffic.

c) Practise on unlit roads where there are a series of hills and bends.

d) Practise on country roads where there are no cats'-eyes.

e) Practise reversing in the dark on both lit and unlit roads.

f) Practise on a narrow country lane with passing places.

g) Practise overtaking on unlit roads.

Common problems

– Fails to notice that it is getting dark

– Forgets to dip headlights when needed

– Dips headlights too late

– Misjudges the speed of oncoming traffic.

– Make sure the learner takes appropriate action when dazzled by another vehicle.

Session 24
Driving in bad weather

Where and when to practise

Practising with learners in bad weather, except in the rain, can be highly dangerous. It is strongly recommended that you should not accompany a learner to drive in adverse weather conditions, other than rain.

In poor weather conditions, learners should only be accompanied by an approved driving instructor in a dual-controlled car. Even then, the conditions may be too dangerous to allow tuition to continue. This Practice Session should not be conducted until the learner has passed the Practical Driving Test and has gained some experience as a newly-qualified driver in good weather conditions.

In the interests of safety, it is further recommended that, whenever possible, newly-qualified drivers should undertake a practical lesson with an approved driving instructor in each bad-weather scenario, before undertaking practice with an accompanying driver.

Planning a practice session

The weather forecast may allow you to plan a bad-weather practice session. You may equally need to seize the opportunity when it arises. In the case of rain and fog, you should plan a route that includes a variety of different types of road both in and out of town. In snow and ice, it is safest to practise car control skills in a large car park or very quiet side roads before driving in traffic.

– Do not practise in snow, ice or fog until the learner has passed the Practical Test.

General safety

– Safety implications are clearly paramount in any practice in bad weather

– Do not attempt to practise in extreme conditions or when organisations like the RAC advise you only to drive if your journey is essential

– Ensure that your car is adequately prepared for the journey

– Carry safety equipment, if appropriate.

Explain what is to be practised and how

The newly-qualified driver will practise driving in one or more of the poor weather scenarios described above. They will practise preparing the car for the journey, using headlights, fog lights, wipers and demisters appropriately, keeping control and maintaining a safe speed.

Check knowledge and understanding

Ask a few questions to check the newly-qualified driver can remember what their driving instructor has taught them about the extra dangers of driving in the specific bad weather conditions they are about to practise. Check in particular that they understand the relationship between a safe speed and visibility and the extra distance it takes to stop in rain, snow and ice. Check also that they understand how to avoid skidding and the principles of skid correction. (See Pass Your Driving Test, pages 65–69.)

Major points to check during practice

The newly-qualified driver:

– checks and prepares the car for the journey

– Make sure the newly-qualified driver uses windscreen wipers, washers and demisters as needed.

- uses lights correctly and turns them off when no longer needed

- uses windscreen wipers, washer and demisters as needed

- drives at an appropriate speed and keeps a safe distance from the vehicle in front

- makes gentle use of the controls and uses appropriate gears for the conditions.

- Does not clear the windscreen of snow or ice adequately before moving off

- Leaves fog lights on when visibility improves.

Advanced exercises

a) Advanced exercises, except in the rain, are too dangerous to practise on a public road.

b) Practise driving in the rain on dual carriageways where spray from large vehicles causes problems.

c) Practise driving in the rain at night.

Common problems

- Drives too fast for the weather conditions

- Drives too close to the vehicle in front

- Uses too low a gear in snow and causes wheelspin

- Forgets to use lights, wipers, windscreen washers, demisters, etc

- Does not check the car before making the journey

Section 3   Practice Sessions
records

Private practice record

On the following pages, you will find a block for each of the 24 BSM Recommended Practice Sessions, with a note of the pages in the book where the session appears. There are up to 4 records per session for you to fill in, but if you require more, use the blank blocks from pages 101–103. Circle the number of the practice for each session, enter the date of the practice and circle any of the Advanced Exercises practised during the session. Finally, make a note of the time spent on each practice session.

We have filled in an example block below for you to use as a guide.

Session 1	Moving off and stopping on a level surface		pages 24–26
Practice No.	Date	Advanced Exercises	Time Spent Practising
①	12/ 11/00	a b ⓒ d	One and a half hours
②	3/ 1 /01	ⓐ b c d	2 hours, 45 minutes
3	/ /	a b c d	
4	/ /	a b c d	

Session 1	Moving off and stopping on a level surface		pages 24–26
Practice No.	Date	Advanced Exercises	Time Spent Practising
1	/ /	a b c d	
2	/ /	a b c d	
3	/ /	a b c d	
4	/ /	a b c d	

Session 2	Using the steering wheel		pages 27–29
Practice No.	Date	Advanced Exercises	Time Spent Practising
1	/ /	a	
2	/ /	a	
3	/ /	a	
4	/ /	a	

Section 3 – Practice Sessions records

Session 3	Clutch control		pages 30–31
Practice No.	Date	Advanced Practice	Time Spent Practising
1	/ /	a b c d	
2	/ /	a b c d	
3	/ /	a b c d	
4	/ /	a b c d	

Session 4	Moving off and stopping uphill		pages 32–34
Practice No.	Date	Advanced Practice	Time Spent Practising
1	/ /	a b c d e	
2	/ /	a b c d e	
3	/ /	a b c d e	
4	/ /	a b c d e	

Session 5	Moving off and stopping downhill		pages 35–37
Practice No.	Date	Advanced Practice	Time Spent Practising
1	/ /	a b c d	
2	/ /	a b c d	
3	/ /	a b c d	
4	/ /	a b c d	

Session 6	Changing up to second and third gear		pages 38–40
Practice No.	Date	Advanced Practice	Time Spent Practising
1	/ /	a b c d	
2	/ /	a b c d	
3	/ /	a b c d	
4	/ /	a b c d	

Session 7	Turning left from a major to a minor road		pages 41–43
Practice No.	Date	Advanced Practice	Time Spent Practising
1	/ /	a b c d e	
2	/ /	a b c d e	
3	/ /	a b c d e	
4	/ /	a b c d e	

Practice Sessions

Session 8	Emerging left from a minor to a major road		pages 44–46
Practice No.	Date	Advanced Practice	Time Spent Practising
1	/ /	a b c d e f g	
2	/ /	a b c d e f g	
3	/ /	a b c d e f g	
4	/ /	a b c d e f g	

Session 9	Turning right from a major to a minor road		pages 47–49
Practice No.	Date	Advanced Practice	Time Spent Practising
1	/ /	a b c d e f	
2	/ /	a b c d e f	
3	/ /	a b c d e f	
4	/ /	a b c d e f	

Session 10	Emerging right from a minor to a major road		pages 50–52
Practice No.	Date	Advanced Practice	Time Spent Practising
1	/ /	a b c d e f g	
2	/ /	a b c d e f g	
3	/ /	a b c d e f g	
4	/ /	a b c d e f g	

Session 11	Changing up and down through all the gears		pages 53–55
Practice No.	Date	Advanced Practice	Time Spent Practising
1	/ /	a b c d e f	
2	/ /	a b c d e f	
3	/ /	a b c d e f	
4	/ /	a b c d e f	

Session 12	Moving off at an angle		pages 56–58
Practice No.	Date	Advanced Practice	Time Spent Practising
1	/ /	a b c d	
2	/ /	a b c d	
3	/ /	a b c d	
4	/ /	a b c d	

Section 3 – Practice Sessions records

Session 13	Reversing around a corner to the left		pages 59–61
Practice No.	Date	Advanced Practice	Time Spent Practising
1	/ /	a b c d e	
2	/ /	a b c d e	
3	/ /	a b c d e	
4	/ /	a b c d e	

Session 14	Reversing around a corner to the right		pages 62–64
Practice No.	Date	Advanced Practice	Time Spent Practising
1	/ /	a b c d e	
2	/ /	a b c d e	
3	/ /	a b c d e	
4	/ /	a b c d e	

Session 15	Turning the car in the road		pages 65–67
Practice No.	Date	Advanced Practice	Time Spent Practising
1	/ /	a b c d e	
2	/ /	a b c d e	
3	/ /	a b c d e	
4	/ /	a b c d e	

Session 16	Reversing into a parking space		pages 68–70
Practice No.	Date	Advanced Practice	Time Spent Practising
1	/ /	a b c d e	
2	/ /	a b c d e	
3	/ /	a b c d e	
4	/ /	a b c d e	

Session 17	Reverse parking		pages 71–73
Practice No.	Date	Advanced Practice	Time Spent Practising
1	/ /	a b c d e	
2	/ /	a b c d e	
3	/ /	a b c d e	
4	/ /	a b c d e	

Practice Sessions

Session 18	Dealing with roundabouts		pages 74–76
Practice No.	Date	Advanced Practice	Time Spent Practising
1	/ /	a b c d e f	
2	/ /	a b c d e f	
3	/ /	a b c d e f	
4	/ /	a b c d e f	

Session 19	Dealing with pedestrian crossings		pages 77–79
Practice No.	Date	Advanced Practice	Time Spent Practising
1	/ /	a b c d e	
2	/ /	a b c d e	
3	/ /	a b c d e	
4	/ /	a b c d e	

Session 20	Meeting other traffic		pages 80–81
Practice No.	Date	Advanced Practice	Time Spent Practising
1	/ /	a b c d	
2	/ /	a b c d	
3	/ /	a b c d	
4	/ /	a b c d	

Session 21	Dealing with dual carriageways		pages 82–84
Practice No.	Date	Advanced Practice	Time Spent Practising
1	/ /	a b c d	
2	/ /	a b c d	
3	/ /	a b c d	
4	/ /	a b c d	

Session 22	Commentary driving		pages 85–87
Practice No.	Date	Advanced Practice	Time Spent Practising
1	/ /	a b c d	
2	/ /	a b c d	
3	/ /	a b c d	
4	/ /	a b c d	

Session 23	Night driving		pages 88–90
Practice No.	Date	Advanced Practice	Time Spent Practising
1	/ /	a b c d e f g	
2	/ /	a b c d e f g	
3	/ /	a b c d e f g	
4	/ /	a b c d e f g	

Session 24 Driving in bad weather			pages 91–93
Practice No.	Date	Advanced Practice	Time Spent Practising
1	/ /	a b c d e	
2	/ /	a b c d e	
3	/ /	a b c d e	
4	/ /	a b c d e	

Session No:	Subject:		
Practice No.	Date	Advanced Practice	Time Spent Practising
1	/ /	a b c d e f g	
2	/ /	a b c d e f g	
3	/ /	a b c d e f g	
4	/ /	a b c d e f g	

Session No:	Subject:		
Practice No.	Date	Advanced Practice	Time Spent Practising
1	/ /	a b c d e f g	
2	/ /	a b c d e f g	
3	/ /	a b c d e f g	
4	/ /	a b c d e f g	

Practice Sessions

Session No: ___	Subject: _____		
Practice No.	Date	Advanced Practice	Time Spent Practising
1	/ /	a b c d e f g	
2	/ /	a b c d e f g	
3	/ /	a b c d e f g	
4	/ /	a b c d e f g	

Session No: ___	Subject: _____		
Practice No.	Date	Advanced Practice	Time Spent Practising
1	/ /	a b c d e f g	
2	/ /	a b c d e f g	
3	/ /	a b c d e f g	
4	/ /	a b c d e f g	

Session No: ___	Subject: _____		
Practice No.	Date	Advanced Practice	Time Spent Practising
1	/ /	a b c d e f g	
2	/ /	a b c d e f g	
3	/ /	a b c d e f g	
4	/ /	a b c d e f g	

Session No: ___	Subject: _____		
Practice No.	Date	Advanced Practice	Time Spent Practising
1	/ /	a b c d e f g	
2	/ /	a b c d e f g	
3	/ /	a b c d e f g	
4	/ /	a b c d e f g	

Session No: ___	Subject: _____		
Practice No.	Date	Advanced Practice	Time Spent Practising
1	/ /	a b c d e f g	
2	/ /	a b c d e f g	
3	/ /	a b c d e f g	
4	/ /	a b c d e f g	

Section 3 – Practice Sessions records

Session No: _____ Subject: _____			
Practice No.	Date	Advanced Practice	Time Spent Practising
1	/ /	a b c d e f g	
2	/ /	a b c d e f g	
3	/ /	a b c d e f g	
4	/ /	a b c d e f g	

Session No: _____ Subject: _____			
Practice No.	Date	Advanced Practice	Time Spent Practising
1	/ /	a b c d e f g	
2	/ /	a b c d e f g	
3	/ /	a b c d e f g	
4	/ /	a b c d e f g	

Session No: _____ Subject: _____			
Practice No.	Date	Advanced Practice	Time Spent Practising
1	/ /	a b c d e f g	
2	/ /	a b c d e f g	
3	/ /	a b c d e f g	
4	/ /	a b c d e f g	

Session No: _____ Subject: _____			
Practice No.	Date	Advanced Practice	Time Spent Practising
1	/ /	a b c d e f g	
2	/ /	a b c d e f g	
3	/ /	a b c d e f g	
4	/ /	a b c d e f g	

Session No: _____ Subject: _____			
Practice No.	Date	Advanced Practice	Time Spent Practising
1	/ /	a b c d e f g	
2	/ /	a b c d e f g	
3	/ /	a b c d e f g	
4	/ /	a b c d e f g